Pebble® Plus

THE U.S. MILITARY BRANCHES

THE U.S. MARINE CORPS

by Jennifer Reed

CAPSTONE PRESS
a capstone imprint

Pebble Plus is published by Capstone Press,
1710 Roe Crest Drive, North Mankato, Minnesota 56003
www.mycapstone.com

Library of Congress Cataloging-in-Publication Data
Names: Reed, Jennifer, 1967- author.
Title: The U.S. Marine Corps / by Jennifer Reed.
Description: North Mankato, Minnesota : Capstone Press, [2018] | Series:
 Pebble plus. The U.S. Marine Corps military branches | Includes
 bibliographical references and index. | Audience: Grades K-3. |
Audience: Ages 4–8.
Identifiers: LCCN 2016052801 | ISBN 9781515767725 (library binding) |
 ISBN 9781515767763 (pbk.) | ISBN 9781515767886 (ebook : .pdf)
Subjects: LCSH: United States. Marine Corps—Juvenile literature.
Classification: LCC VE23 .R44 2018 | DDC 359.9/60973—dc23
LC record available at https://lccn.loc.gov/2016052801

Editorial Credits
Nikki Bruno Clapper, editor; Kayla Dohmen, designer; Jo Miller, media researcher;
Laura Manthe, production specialist

Image Credits
U.S. Marine Corps photo by Cpl. Alejandro Pena, 5, Cpl. Hernan Vidana, 1, Lance Cpl.
Alexander Hill, cover, Lance Cpl. Cristian L. Ricardo, 21, Pfc. Sandra Garduno, 7, Sgt. Brytani
Wheeler, 17, Sgt. Gregory Moore, 3rd MAW Combat Camera, 15, Sgt. Sarah Anderson, 13, Lance
Cpl. Devan Gowans, 9, Cpl. Abraham Lopez, MAWTS-1 COMCAM, 11; U.S. Navy photo by
Mass Communication Specialist 3rd Class Shawnte Bryan, 19

Design Elements
Shutterstock: Aqua, DmitriyRazinkov, Kolonko, Marisha. Omelchenko

Note to Parents and Teachers

The U.S. Military Branches set supports national curriculum standards for science related to
science, technology, and society. This book describes and illustrates the U.S. Marine Corps. The
images support early readers in understanding the text. The repetition of words and phrases
helps early readers learn new words. This book also introduces early readers to subject-specific
vocabulary words, which are defined in the Glossary section. Early readers may need assistance
to read some words and to use the Table of Contents, Glossary, Read More, Internet Sites,
Critical Thinking Questions, and Index sections of the book.

Printed in China.
010322F17

TABLE OF CONTENTS

Ready to Fight

The Marine Corps
is a branch of the
United States Armed Forces.
Marines are often the first
branch to fight in battles.

Marines can fight anywhere.
They battle on land, at sea,
or in the air. Marines often
help the U.S. Navy.

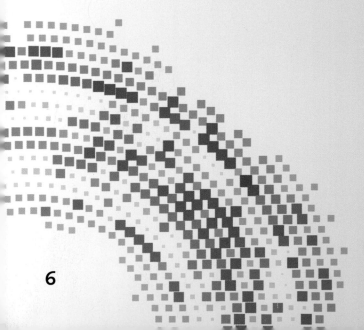

Marine Corps Jobs

Marine pilots fly planes
and helicopters. The MV-22
Osprey can carry 24 Marines.
It takes off straight up
into the sky.

Infantry Marines fight
on the ground. Musicians
play in the Marine band.
Other Marines take pictures
of battles.

Machines and Weapons

Marines use many vehicles. The AAV-7 moves on water and on land. The MTVR is a truck. It carries people and supplies.

an AAV-7

The F/A-18 Hornet is
a Marine fighter jet.
It drops missiles and
bombs on enemy targets.

The Blackjack is a drone.
It flies without a pilot. It has
a video camera. Marines look
at the videos to see what
is happening. They stay safe.

Marines also use weapons. They fight with M-4 and M-16 rifles. Grenades and missiles blow up targets.

M-4 rifles

For Their Country

Marines fight all over
the world. They risk their
lives for their country.

Glossary

AAV—assault amphibian vehicle; AAVs can float on water and travel on land

Armed Forces—the whole military; the U.S. Armed Forces include the Army, Navy, Air Force, Marine Corps, and Coast Guard

battle—a fight between two military groups

binoculars—a tool that makes far-away objects look closer

branch—a part of a larger group

drone—an unmanned, remote-controlled aircraft or missile

grenade—a small bomb that can be thrown or launched

missile—an explosive weapon that is thrown or shot at a distant target

rifle—a long-barreled gun that is fired from the shoulder

target—an object at which to aim or shoot

vehicle—a machine that carries people and goods

Read More

Callery, Sean. *Branches of the Military*. Discover More Readers. New York: Scholastic, 2015.

Marx, Mandy R. *Amazing U.S. Marine Facts*. Amazing Military Facts. North Mankato, Minn.: Capstone Press, 2017.

Murray, Julie. *United States Marine Corps*. U.S. Armed Forces. Minneapolis: Abdo Kids, 2015.

Internet Sites

FactHound offers a safe, fun way to find Internet sites related to this book. All of the sites on FactHound have been researched by our staff.

Here's all you do:
Visit *www.facthound.com*
Type in this code: 9781515767725

Super-cool stuff!

Check out projects, games and lots more at
www.capstonekids.com

Critical Thinking Questions

1. What do you think Marines are trained to do well?

2. What is a battle? How do Marines stay ready for battle?

3. What tools do Marines carry? How do these tools help them?

Index